just remember you're beautiful

madison rose

about me

introductions are boring unless you're telling me your whole life story, so i guess what im trying to say is let me try and tell you my whole story in one breath. my name is madison rose, im 21 years old, i am a triplet and since you may ask... we are two girls and one boy. our birthday falls on christmas eve. no. we don't get double presents. we get a couple on our birthday and on christmas. which does not count as double in my book. blah blah anyways.

i love that word so much i have it tattooed on me (anyways) lovely word. i have 39 tattoos well if you're reading this in the near future I may have 100s. "near future" as in maybe a couple days from myself writing this. lol. here's a couple more facts and then we can get juicy.

speaking of juicy. i have a golden retriever named juice. my all time favorite movie franchise is harry potter. i listen to the soundtrack and watch the movies daily. listening to it right now actually!

this book is all my feelings in one. from the best days to the worst days of my life. this book, this story means so much to me in so many ways I can't describe. ive cried writing some and smiled or giggled writing others. and I hope you can too. whether you relate by sending it to a friend or just feel it yourself. my whole heart is in this book and i hope you can take care of it how you would your own. remember that this is "just a book" so, whether you open it now or later the meaning of it is not going anywhere and neither am i. you might not ever relate or you might relate too much and both are okay.

i want you to write on me. take a picture of my pages. fold over one you like so you can reread it non-stop. highlight something that catches your eye. and more. these are your pages as much as they are mine. don't ever be afraid to relate to something that you wish you didn't have to. you're not "just a person" you're someone's best friend, someone's light, someone's smile, and reason for still being here. that's my favorite thing about you.

i love you. enjoy. <3<3<3<3<3

~ *Madison Rose*

just remember you're beautiful

madison rose

eyes

I stand in front of you
and with you
as I open my eyes,
see through them,
see what I see
trees; they change as humans
do.
You see fruit,
you don't know when they
were planted, you don't know
where they came from, you
don't know their journey, you
don't know how they feel or
what they have gone through
(their past) isn't yours.
don't judge
Just watch and listen, see from
a distance, and talk from afar. I
walk with you, I hear, I protect,
I believe, receive in love, or
think again

I love you
Luv u 2

I'm scared to love again or, more
so, to be loved
I can't remember if being loved
even feels good because of how
bad it was
and how much I didn't hate it in
the moment, but something about
you felt right
the feeling of love, I think, is so
wrong that maybe I'm afraid of
how I didn't know

As much as I hate to argue,
last night was okay
with you,
I feel safe.
It upset me the way we spoke,
the way we felt,
and the way I woke. I'm not sure
where we lay but if it's with you,
I think I'm okay to say
as long as it's you,
there's nothing more that I want
than to look at your face and say
that I love you

there's so much stuff going through my mind, yet nothing at all because when I look at you, I fall, into a deep sleep of love in your eyes, I see something different, yet I hear what you say, and I've heard it before, but this time I can't stop wanting it more because when I look at you, I fall into a deep sleep of love. The pain I used to feel made my heart numb, yet all you do is sum up the feeling I've wanted to feel for a while except I think yours is real

They're all the same. Am I stupid?
Drive me insane, you did.
Fill my heart with pain, crumble me
up
like a piece of paper, shred my heart
just like him. fuck! Am I stupid?
no
you're just used to it

I love looking at you; your eyes are ocean blue. I love looking at you; it's all I ever do. I love looking at you. It gives me butterflies when I stare. I love looking at you. Oh, how much I care. I love looking at you I can't take my gaze off you. I love looking at you

Oh, how much I wish you knew I love looking at you. Your lips are so soft.
I love looking at you.
You make time stop. I love looking at you the way it makes me feel. I love looking at you. Oh, how my heart heals. I love looking at you and how you make me feel. I love looking at you; it's been a while since I found someone so pure at heart. I love looking at you; you're my favorite piece of art.

There's nothing more embarrassing than the feeling of hope

talk
I've been broken before, but I've put it in a sock
one wrong turn and that's one step forward,
five steps back to block my insecurities; hurt
me to push you away can only carry
sometimes, it feels like forever; I feel invisible
smother?
Me?
Could you hold me?
just look at me if you wish to feel the feeling of
importance without having to grasp at crumbs
that are given to look me in my eyes for only 7
seconds sometimes I feel
I have to do it first, and if I don't, it just gets
worse my insecurities hurt

I'm my biggest fear

we may not be here forever, but did you (ever) realize that you're here (for) a reason & life? Well
life may sound overrated sometimes, but I promise you you're just overthinking because, in reality, that's reality. Live in faith equally

222

i love you baby
how was your day:)

.. i love you more
sweetheart
... it was so good but
it's better with you
how was yours?

it was great but like
you said, better with
you

... i miss you so
much come over i
want to cuddle

okay im on my way i
miss you so much
more

...yay drive safe baby
i will see you soon
<3 i love you

i love you

hey baby how was
your day

                      ... good you?

mine was good but
better with you :)

                      ...

wyd honey <3

                      ...

well im laying in bed,
just got done eating
missin you :)

                  ...chillin

okay well i'm going
to bed i love you
goodnight

                  ... night love u

My world has completely stopped; all I care about is you. I care about you
more than I care about myself, I live for other people, burry mistakes and red flags I hide behind the shadows; life lags One lay in lies.
lies I tell myself I'm not pretty how I'm boring that no one cares about me, say my well-being is pointless and careless.
forgiveness
I forgive everyone who has hurt me like it's the right thing to do, yet when we forgive someone, maybe too soon?

You're not even real
I dreamt you, and I made you up, a fantasy.
I can't feel you, see you, hear you love is
such a bad thing
our minds and bodies convince us
otherwise so we don't feel so bad about the
abuse, just like an addiction; crying for no
reason is the reason I'm crying
when I know or should have known you'd be
just like them, the only difference you had
was convincing me a little more that you
weren't that way, a bad guy, I say convinced
me better than he did

i feel sad

i'm lost

in a field entire of flowers id pick you first, they said you are a red
flower in a white flower field, you stand out to me the most; you stand so confident and pretty; you cost
through the Wind, you're so colorful and witty people compliment you all the time oh, how gorgeous you are they smell you and admire you but never get to know you; they touch your petals and leaves
but don't care enough to love you, but they keep on sniffing till there's something new
in a field entire of flowers id pick you

I hate you he says
I love you she says
you're annoying,
he says you're
funny, she says
you're stupid, he
says you're smart,
she says shut up,
he says okay she
says he's okay, he
says she cries
instead
he ponders and
wonders with his
eyes so big
to only remember
what he did
I'm sorry he says
she's quiet in bed
take me back, he
said the silence
grew big I love you
he says
to only find a note
that read oh, to be
yours, she said
how wonderful it
must be.
I may be stupid,
but I can see the
way it was is
beyond the sea
and that's where
I'll find my man to
be you said you
loved me, oh, do
you now?
I've had enough,
she said
I'll see you around.

HOT

CUTE

SEXY

FUNNY

KIND

LOVING

Someone once told me
I want to show you what love is,
but only to show me what it isn't
yet. I'm starting to believe maybe it
is like this because of how many
people told me this: I love you so
much; you're so beautiful; here's a
couple of flowers,
watch love overpower, and hours
pass by with the same ending sigh
you didn't hear me; it's just the
beginning one more time this time;
listen to me. I love you so much;
you said
you're the love of my life, you said I
want to marry you
You said, and you said, and you
said, but in tiny writing, it read
someone who loves you wouldn't
have said they would have done it
instead. Now, did you hear me?

lost confused
it's just something I'm used to; my mind constantly
spins circles, and I never win
I dreamt it would be you rest your eyes the hardest
goodbyes lost

333

confused
understood muse. Do you believe this poem
has no value but to me? I do.
It may just be words that make no sense, but
they sound pretty together,
I guess

Chasing cars, chasing me, and chasing my reflection isn't easy, They say to love yourself first before loving something else, as if falling in love cancels. Cancels out the feeling of pain. Pain is something that sits with you, an emotion that comes and goes that's just how it flows under pressure, or utterly okay pain is something that will always stay

I never thought love could hurt more than real pain; crazy insane. I'm in pain. Your words hurt, yet I'm insane. You call me names. You say I'm mentally ill; I stand still you look me in the eyes and tell me I'm dumb. You call me a ball & chain, yet I'm insane you shove me and hit me, and you're in pain? Oh, right, but I'm insane. I stayed with you because I was comfortable, so I looked in the mirror and couldn't remember my name. I never thought love could hurt more than actual pain. Insane

We're not meant to be. Oh the way
the way you look at me, we're not
meant to be. Oh, the way the way you
hold me, we're not meant to be. Oh,
the way the way you know me, we're
not meant to be. Oh, the way the way
you laugh with me, we are meant to
be, oh, the way the way you hurt me,
we are meant to be, oh, the way the
way you speak to me, we are meant
to be, oh, the way the way you yell at
me
we're meant to be or not to be, you'll
always see me as the enemy we're
only meant to be when it's not easy
I'm only meant to be with the idea of
what you could be

Not how it should be. I'm meant
for someone who can treat me
the way I'm supposed to be, not
the hallucination I see to ease
just so I don't cry myself to sleep

I stare at the wall at nothing at all. My eyes are blank; I don't blink, frozen in time

I'm numb in the spine, with no feeling in my body as I stare at this wall, yet I'm not staring at all. I'm blank-faced with no emotion placed. It's a good stare, I say. While I play our memories in my head like a dream as if I'm lying in   bed.

Numb, I stare at the wall but at nothing   at   all.

world of yours i
only see you when i close my eyes
all the highs.

the cycle never ends...
the feeling of pain
inside my head
I wish you'd just hit me
instead
cuddle me, love me,
hear me, feel me, hurt
me, kill me, the cycle
never ends. I let it slide
to hurt myself to die
leave him to the side,
move on with your life,
forget the feeling
inside, kiss me, hold
me, tell me you love
me is the feeling and
cycle I wish to
remember

Not every bee that lands in your garden is here to stay. They might take a nap in your flower, maybe stay for a little chat, only to stab you in the back
take what's most important from you as if they didn't know that the only thing keeping you standing now has a hole

when i needed to be
watered i didn't
mean make me cry

i'm falling in love

in
love
with
you

444

The truth will always be set free
because the truth did nothing wrong

"I promise I will never be like them,"
you promised, and I trusted you;
believe me, I knew that maybe one
day you'd forget
that you promised me on the day
we met filled with the butterfly
feeling like the effect.
It affects how I see you. I wish you
knew. that when you promised, I
believed you
and somehow, I still do

nothing

Why is it so easy for you to walk away? Is it me, my face, my acne, or my weight? Huh, what is it? Just tell me, please, I'll fix it, and you'll love me then, right? Please, oh please, oh, tell me why, but don't lie, I'll change for you. Be the perfect person to tell me what to change. That's all you have to do, and if I do it right and change it for you, I'll be good as new. Will you love me then, or tell me you do

hey you.
i love you.

If I don't talk about how I feel,
it will kill me faster by eating
me alive
from the silence, I feed it

my heart's
too big
it holds all
the wrong
feelings

Oh, how I'm drawn to you. I can't take my eyes off you when I look at you; that's all I'd ever want to do. Oh, how I'm drawn to you, the way you laugh, your smile
Oh, it's been a while since I found someone like you

I talk about my past as if it's something I like to talk about it's the hardest thing to talk about

No matter how heavy the weight is,
it will always make you feel stronger

555

They claim they once loved you,
but they didn't fight to stay

I wrote about our future. We talked about our house and how we wanted it to look. We talked about the bathroom style and how we wanted a book
nook, a library full of books we'll never read, and maybe an eight-car garage for the cars we don't need. We talked about our future and all our children's names. You told me you loved me, which is all you claimed, but you walked away without thinking of our future, not a tear down your face. You forgot about our love and all our children's names. I wrote about our future, thinking you would stay, except you left without warning on a random day

What I hate the most
is I feel like everyone
disregards my
feelings yet I went
through it, too

I haven't thought of you today
and well, I haven't thought of you at all.
It's as if my mind is trying to forget you,
and my heart is letting it happen. I miss
the way you'd look at me; I miss the
way you'd touch me
And now I barely remember you at all.
The way your laugh sounds when I tell a
funny joke, the way your warmth
radiates off your skin when I hug you, I
can't even remember how you smell,
and sometimes I pass the places we
used to go, and I can't even remember
how long ago that was.

There's nothing more I want
than to give you those
butterfly kisses and those
head scratches all night long,
but how can someone do
such a thing when you aren't
here at all
I want to remember you, but
it's just something I can no
longer do and the saddest
part about all of this
is how I can't even
remember the way I looked
at you

I cry so much that I start to feel like I'm floating as if I'm moving with the current it's going the wrong way

Being numb is hard to explain in words that mean something, so listen carefully as I tell you what it means. It's an emptiness that fills you, a void that can't be filled, a feeling of detachment from everything that's real. You may feel tons of emotion or cry for no reason, but it will all make sense, so listen. The pain of being numb is a pain that's hard to bear. It's a pain that's all-consuming, and it's always there, but there's a glimmer of hope and a light that shines within. If you keep searching for it, you'll find it and the feeling of life again. You will feel such things becoming a whole. To be free, the pain of numbness will be a distant memory.

You love them for who they are and everything you can see, except they don't know,
so you're left with just a fantasy. You want to tell them how you feel, but you're afraid of what they'll say, so you stare at them with happiness, hoping they notice one day

You practice what you'll say and talk about them all day, but they must not feel the same cause when you look their way, they don't even know your name. I love them for who they are, but I think it's best if I love them from afar

i made a decision off of how I felt
from a broken heart, but it didn't help

broken hearted is the worst type of
pain but have you ever felt your mind
go insane

When you put my heart back together, i didn't know you were going to break it too

I thought of an idea with the art of falling in love, but you painted over the picture with a push and a shove.

Then there was a destroyed and unloved picture, so I painted it again to cover it up.

what   broke
me;   was
realizing   they
were   looking
past   me   the
whole   time

you are
strong you
are funny
you are
kind and
you are
loving you
are bold
and
contagious
you make
me smile
through all
the pages

you said i was perfect

don't be afraid of
what it could be

You use me like I'm liquor,
just a body and a figure
you fill me up drink me
again
just for me to sit there you
empty my soul like alcohol
plays a role.
I wish I could unscroll.
Here we go again.
The cycle never ends
I'll sit there as you use me
while I don't consent

Love is like a dream, a vision, or a
distant memory. It's a feeling oh so
pure; it's something we can't ignore.
Oh, we must adore it. It's like a stream
that flows so smoothly it's free and has
no will. It glides; it's never still
patient and full of laughter.

It's a gentle kind, and all that
matters love that's good can be
hard
take every moment with all your
heart. Love is fun; love is great.
Remember your first date, the
butterfly you felt, and how you
wanted more. Remember that
love is something to adore.

I asked my partner
What would they write if I passed
away?

They responded with nothing.
I would write nothing.
I asked why. They said because I would
be right there with you, life isn't worth
living without you right next to me

our life is
like a
story my
favorite
book to
read let's
finish
this book
together
that is all
i need

everything's gonna be okay

you're my favorite person

the best part of me was you

777

putting a price on emotion is
hard when you can cry for free

If my life were a picture book, I would return to your chapter to see you again. I'd read all the pages just to listen to your jokes and stupid stories, and I'd do it all over again without even trying

is your past a ghost?
then don't let it haunt you

ill always love you

what was i thinking

One of the most incredible things in life is living.
Just living.
Life is no movie, not a TV show or a play, but it's yours, and you can write it however you want, but you can't rewind that scene. You can't pause it and finish it later.
You can slow down and take your time but don't just stop and never finish your story. Remember that yours is the most important one.

i want you here

Healing is a journey that allows you to mend your broken pieces. It's something we do to find ways to forgive and forget. It helps us see ourselves and grow. We learn from our mistakes and talk about how we feel or felt.

Healing is sometimes all we need to feel at peace. So, find that time to heal. Find the space in your heart and mind to release the bad and the pain from the past. Replace that feeling with good and love. And heal your soul from within and above.

I fear my own words, and you
can't catch a break.
I'm afraid
to push you away.
The feeling of overthinking is
like the feeling of a mistake
to push you away
is the last thing I want to do,
so please stay with me as I do
my best to understand you

When your charger is broken and it only works at an angle, we wrap it and fold it around the phone to make it work but sometimes it won't work at that angle, and it will stop working on the fold, so we finally have to say goodbye and move on to a better one put that into the perspective of love you can keep trying to fix something broken and do things to make it work.

it may be hard to get it right each time, but if it works and you have no issues doing so, then do it but sometimes, it will eventually just give out so you can either try and fix something that's broken or let go but know you'll have to move on at some point.

888

People are too busy living their lives to realize you had a bad day. If you sigh, you're annoying. If you whine, you're a baby. If you cry, you're sensitive. If you sleep, you're depressed.
But you only wanted someone to notice without making it known first.

happy endings don't always end with love

but they do exist

I'm sitting in the car, smiling at your smile. You're looking into my eyes, not saying anything. I look away to giggle. I can't help but smile I turned back, and you weren't there. You disappeared.
I reminisce, feeling like you were still here.

i like how
ordinary
you are it
screams
different

crying in my pillow gives me
dreams about the ocean

i compare myself to my reflection
cause even shes prettier than me

she's more than love.

when i gave myself scars you
signed your name beneath them

when we said it was over, I didn't
know my thoughts would hold
onto you I tried to forget you,
but the memories couldn't be
lost. They were saved in files too
far away. I'm exhausted. I
wanted to find the guy who was
kind when I wanted the right
love. You stood there and sighed
it was something we did all the
time. You begged for
forgiveness, and although I cried
I tell myself to remember you as
the guy who was kind

Time is not the future
Time goes forward and then
starts all over again
Time only heals when you wait
Time only tells when it's fate
Time is perfect
Not
Perfect timing
Time will always be right
Never
Right on Time
Time is the most hopeless yet
valuable thing
Ugh
Today is going by slowly. Or
Today went by so fast
Interesting right
Time is, well, Time is not past.
Time is forward. It will always
last.
Times, not a race,
It's just something that will
never lose pace
Sure, daylight savings
set the clock "forward" and set
the time "back."
The same clock ticks
And the same Time will never
be still, So either get up and
do something Or that Time
will kill
Time does not define you
Time is just Time
So you could sit there all you
want And wait for Time to pass
Just remember time moves
forward
So you may just come in last

999

just remember youre beautiful

fin.

MADISON ROSE

About the author

Madison Rose was born on December 24th, 2002, in Phoenix, Arizona. Madison found an interest in poetry in grade school when assigned a project to create a book for class, but never went further than that. She then later found an urge for writing, which is quite funny considering she's not a huge fan of reading. Today she is probably laying in bed... kidding, she is proceeding with her passions aside from writing. Madison's first book to ever be published is the one you are reading right now :) Yes, the one in your hand. Yep, this one. "just remember youre beautiful."

e9be9d92-3e9c-4a8d-823d-a992cf9a384dR01